Fun and Festive SUMMER CRAFTS

Fun and Festive Crafts for the Seasons

Tie-Dyed Shirts, Bug Cages, and Sand Castles

Randel McGee

Enslow Elementary

an imprint of

Enslow Publishers, Inc.

40 Industrial Road
Box 398
Berkeley Heights, NJ 07922
USA

www.enslow.com

Dedicated to Mable, Greta, and James Evans

Enslow Elementary, an imprint of Enslow Publishers, Inc.

Enslow Elementary® is a registered trademark of Enslow Publishers, Inc.

Library of Congress Cataloging-in-Publication Data

McGee, Randel.
    Fun and festive summer crafts : tie-dyed shirts, bug cages, and sand castles / Randel McGee.
        pages cm. — (Fun and festive crafts for the seasons)
    Summary: "Includes the scientific explanation behind the summer season, a related myth, and step-by-step
        instructions on how to make eight summer-themed crafts out of various materials"— Provided by publisher.
    Audience: Grades 4 to 6.
    Includes bibliographical references and index.
    ISBN 978-0-7660-4319-0 — ISBN 978-1-4644-0583-9 (paperback) — ISBN 978-1-4645-1281-0 (ePUB) —
        ISBN 978-1-4646-1281-7 (single-user PDF) — ISBN 978-0-7660-5913-9 (multi-user PDF) 1. Handicraft—
        Juvenile literature. 2. Summer—Juvenile literature. I. Title.
    TT160.M3849 2015
    745.5—dc23

                2013028061

Future editions:
Paperback ISBN: 978-1-4644-0583-9   EPUB ISBN: 978-1-4645-1281-0
Single-User PDF ISBN: 978-1-4646-1281-7   Multi-User PDF ISBN: 978-0-7660-5913-9

Printed in the United States of America

052014 Lake Book Manufacturing, Inc., Melrose Park, IL

10 9 8 7 6 5 4 3 2 1

To Our Readers: We have done our best to make sure all Internet addresses in this book were active and appropriate when we went to press. However, the author and the publisher have no control over and assume no liability for the material available on those Internet sites or on other Web sites they may link to. Any comments or suggestions can be sent by e-mail to comments@enslow.com or to the address on the back cover.

♻ Enslow Publishers, Inc., is committed to printing our books on recycled paper. The paper in every book contains 10% to 30% post-consumer waste (PCW). The cover board on the outside of each book contains 100% PCW. Our goal is to do our part to help young people and the environment too!

Photo Credits: Crafts prepared by Randel McGee and p. 48; craft photography by Enslow Publishers, Inc.; Designua/ Shutterstock.com, p. 5.

Cover photo: Crafts prepared by Randel McGee; photography by Enslow Publishers, Inc.

Contents

AUTHOR'S NOTE: The projects in this book were created for this particular season. However, I invite readers to be imaginative and find new ways to use the ideas in this book to create different projects of their own. Please feel free to share pictures of your work with me through www.mcgeeproductions.com. Happy crafting!

Summer!

Legends say that long, long ago in Hawaii, there lived a clever man named Maui (MAH-oo-EE). His mother, Hina (HEE-nah), complained to him that the sun ran across the sky so quickly, she did not have time to make her special kapa cloth and let it dry before it was dark. Maui's friends also complained that they could not get all their work done before it was too dark to see. Maui decided that he would just have to make the sun slow down. He made magic ropes of woven coconut fibers and climbed to the top of Mt. Haleakala (HAH-lay-ah-KAH-lah) near the sun's home. When the sun started to stretch his sunbeam leg over the mountain, Maui threw the rope around it and tied it to the mountain. He did this again and again until the sun's many legs were trapped.

The sun cried to be set free, but Maui said he would not set the sun free until he promised to go slower as he crossed the sky. The sun struggled and fought against the ropes, but he could not get loose. Finally, the sun agreed to slow down his daily journey across the sky during half of the year. Maui let him go and the sun kept his promise. This is how the long days of summer came to be.

This is a fantastic adventure story, but what really causes the longer days of summer is that Earth is tilted slightly from north to south. During the summer months, the Northern Hemisphere, the top half of Earth, leans closer to the sun. The Northern Hemisphere receives more light and heat than the Southern Hemisphere. When the sun reaches its highest point on the Northern Hemisphere, it is called the summer solstice. *Solstice* comes from a Latin word that means "where the sun stops." June 21 is usually the day of the summer solstice, where the sun shines as far north as it can before Earth starts to lean the other way. The summer solstice has the longest daylight hours of the year. A summer solstice in the north means it is the winter solstice in the south.

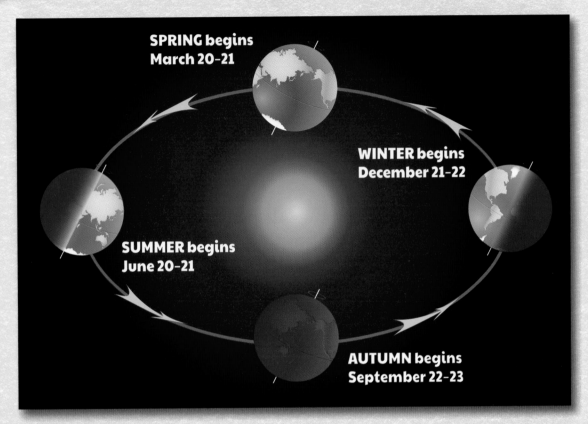

SPRING begins
March 20–21

WINTER begins
December 21–22

SUMMER begins
June 20–21

AUTUMN begins
September 22–23

The longer days of summer give people extra time to do things outside, such as playing games and sports, swimming, fishing, chasing butterflies and fireflies, enjoying fresh fruits and vegetables, and having picnics and barbecues. In the United States, there are three special holidays during this season. Memorial Day, the last Monday of May, is the day to honor those who have served their country. It is considered the beginning of summer because most schools close for summer vacation soon after this day. July 4 is a national holiday celebrating Independence Day with parades, picnics, outdoor games and activities, and firework displays. Labor Day is celebrated on the first Monday of September as a day to honor those who have worked hard to make their country successful. It usually marks the end of summer vacation and the beginning of the school year.

Watermelon Refrigerator Magnet

One of the joys of summer is the fresh fruit and vegetables that you can find in the grocery store, farmers' markets, and your own garden. Melons are members of the cucumber family that produce large, sweet fruits. There are many kinds of melons in different colors, sizes, and shapes: round orange cantaloupes; light green honeydews; and the popular oval red watermelon. Use this watermelon refrigerator magnet to post your summer artwork, postcards, and invitations.

What you will need:

- scissors
- craft foam—red, white, and green
- pencil
- permanent markers
- glue
- small magnets or magnet strips

WHAT TO DO:

1. Print and cut out the patterns from page 39. Use pencil or marker to trace them onto the craft foam. The green piece will be the largest, the white piece the next largest, and the red the smallest of the pattern pieces.

#1

2. Cut out the pattern pieces.

#2

3. Glue the pattern pieces on top of each other going from the largest on the bottom to the smallest on the top. Make sure that the top edges match. Let the glue dry.

4. Draw a few dark seeds on the red part with the permanent marker.

#4

5. Glue a small magnet or piece of magnetic strip to the back of the watermelon (on the green side).

#5

PERMANENT SAND CASTLE

In the summer, it is fun to play at the beach of a lake or ocean. The wet sand of a beach can be molded and piled to make sand castles. Many beaches hold contests to see what kinds of sand castles or sculptures people can make. However, you cannot take a sand castle home with you to play with….Or can you? Here is a project that uses cardboard boxes and tubes to make a little "sand" castle that you can play with outside all summer long.

WHAT YOU WILL NEED:

- plastic sheet or garbage bag
- cardboard boxes and tubes of different sizes and shapes
- craft knife (optional)
- light cardboard
- scissors
- glue
- glue wash (½ glue, ½ water)
- paintbrush
- sand
- disposable cup

WHAT TO DO:

#2

1. Spread a plastic sheet or garbage bag over your work area outside to help with cleanup.

2. **Have an adult** use the craft knife to cut windows and doors in the cardboard boxes and tubes as you wish. There are patterns for other castle parts on page 41. Decorate the castle with pieces of light cardboard.

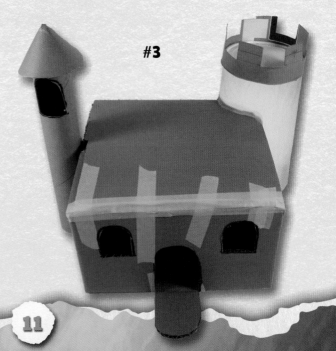

#3

3. Glue the boxes and tubes together to form a castle with towers. Let the glue dry.

4. Make a glue wash by mixing water with the white glue, one part glue and one part water.

5. Paint a section of the castle with a thin layer of the glue wash and use the disposable cup to sprinkle clean sand on that section. Let it dry.

#5

6. Repeat Step 5 for other sections of the castle until the whole castle is covered with a thin layer of sand.

7. Keep the castle in a dry place outside to play with.

#6

Poster Board Hand Fan

Summer can be HOT! Any little breeze helps you feel cooler and more comfortable! You can make your own little breeze with a hand fan. The earliest record of a hand fan is found in Egypt in ancient pictures. Hand fans can be very beautiful and made of very fine materials, or they can be simple and fun. Not only do the fans provide some cooling comfort, but they can also chase away insects that bother people while they try to relax in the heat.

What you will need:

- scissors
- poster board
- pencil
- permanent markers
- poster paints and paintbrushes (optional)
- construction paper (optional)
- glue
- a paint stir stick (found in paint and hardware stores)

WHAT TO DO:

1. Print and cut out the pattern from page 44. Use pencil or marker to trace it onto the poster board.

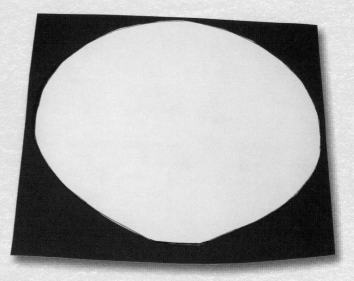

#1

2. Cut out the pattern from the poster board.

3. Use paints, markers, and/or construction paper to decorate one side of the fan with names, flowers, bugs, holiday themes, sports pictures, summer activities, or anything you wish.

#3

4. Glue the paint stir stick to the center of the blank side of the fan. Let it dry.

#4

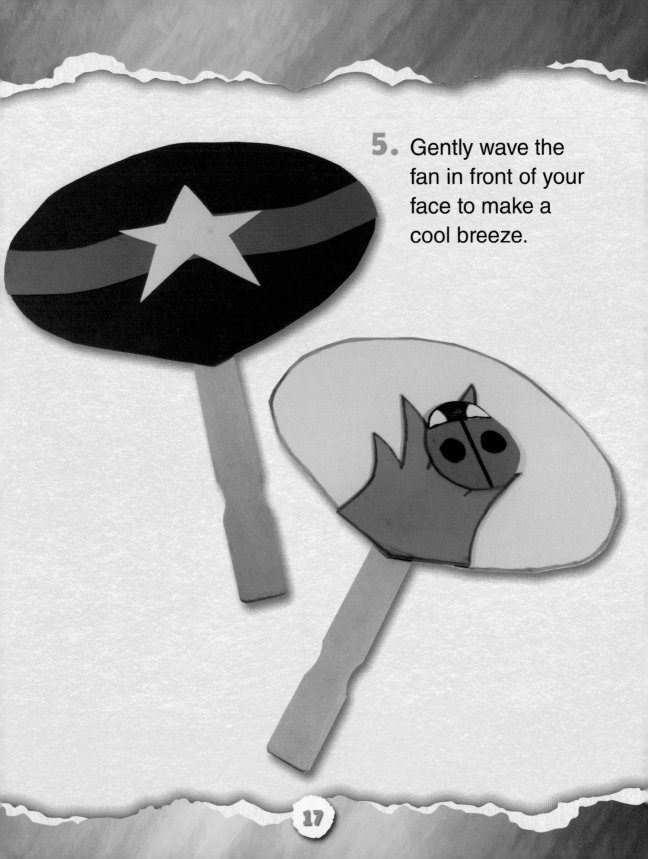

5. Gently wave the fan in front of your face to make a cool breeze.

BUG MASK

Summertime is bug time! Insects are most active during the warm days and nights of summer. Butterflies and bees collect flower nectars all day. Ants want to try our picnic foods. At night, moths and June bugs buzz around outside lights by the dozens! Have you ever wondered what it would be like to be a bug? With this mask, you and your friends can make up skits to share or just have fun pretending to be bugs.

WHAT YOU WILL NEED:

- scissors
- craft foam—9 x 12 inches, different colors
- pencil
- permanent markers
- glue

- acrylic paints and paintbrushes (optional)
- duct tape (optional)
- yarn

WHAT TO DO:

1. Print and cut out the pattern from page 42. Use pencil or marker to trace it onto the craft foam.

#1

2. Cut out the pattern following the solid black lines.

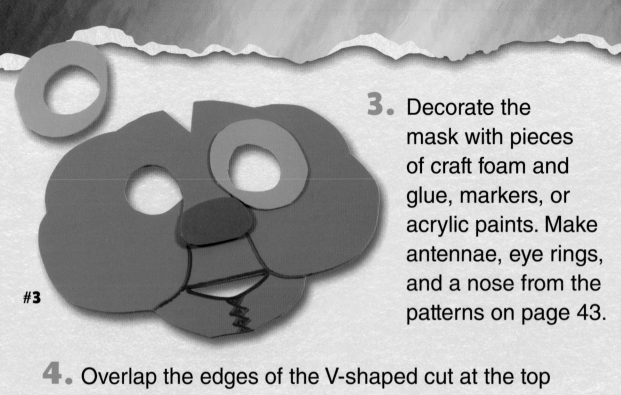

3. Decorate the mask with pieces of craft foam and glue, markers, or acrylic paints. Make antennae, eye rings, and a nose from the patterns on page 43.

#3

4. Overlap the edges of the V-shaped cut at the top of the mask a little and glue or tape them together. Let the glue dry.

5. Cut two 12-inch pieces of yarn and glue or tape them on the inside of the mask close to the eyeholes. Let the glue dry.

#5

6. Gently place the mask on your face and **have an adult** tie the yarn behind your head so that it holds comfortably.

BUG CAGE

Bugs are the most numerous creatures on the planet. Some insects cause trouble by destroying crops and buildings or spreading germs. Other insects are helpful by helping crops to grow, eating harmful bugs, and making honey. Some bugs can fly, dig, swim, jump, or glow in the dark! You can make your own bug cage to be able to watch these interesting creatures up close. Be sure to let the insect go when you have completed your observations.

WHAT YOU WILL NEED:

- a large clear plastic container or jar
- dish soap
- water
- paper towels
- scissors
- craft knife (optional)
- apple slices (optional)
- fresh local plants
- live, harmless insects or plastic insects
- construction paper
- permanent markers
- tape

WHAT TO DO:

1. **Ask an adult** to help. Clean out a large plastic container or jar with warm water and dish soap. Rinse it well. Dry the container with paper towels.

2. **Have an adult** make some holes in the lid of the container with the scissors or the craft knife. Two or three small holes will be enough to let air in without letting the bugs escape.

#2

3. Put a damp paper towel and a small apple slice in the container. This provides enough moisture for the bugs to be comfortable and some food for them.

#3

4. Take the container outside. Put some fresh plants inside, making sure that the lid will still close properly. Put in just enough plant material for the bugs to climb on but not so much that you can't see the bugs.

#4

5. Safely and gently capture some harmless types of insects and put them in the container and set the lid on tightly. Only capture one insect at a time. Some examples of insects that are rather easy to catch and harmless are ladybugs, fireflies, grasshoppers, moths, and caterpillars. **Note:** If you do not want to catch live insects you may want to display some plastic bugs.

6. Use the construction paper, scissors, and markers to make little signs to identify each insect. Tell a bit about its life and when it was found. Tape the signs to the top of your cage.

Praying Mantis
Insecta – Mantodea
It looks like he's praying.
It eats other insects.
I found it on a rose-bush in my yard.

#6

7. After you have enjoyed watching the bug for a day, let it go free, and replace it with a new bug. **Note:** If a caterpillar starts to make a cocoon or chrysalis (a hard shell like a cocoon) you may want to keep it in a safe place outside until it becomes a moth or butterfly.

STAMPED PENNANT

A pennant is a long triangle-shaped flag. Pennants have been used for centuries to send signals over short distances; as symbols for royalty, armies, or sports teams; and as decorations. The word *pennant* comes from the Latin word *penna* which means "wing" because they flutter in the wind. Your summer sporting event, holiday, or picnic will look festive with a string of brightly colored pennants as decoration!

WHAT YOU WILL NEED:

* scissors
* craft foam—½-inch thick, any color
* pencil
* craft knife (optional)
* waterproof glue
* scraps of wood at least 3 x 3 inches on one side
* linen cloth, bulletin board paper, or butcher paper
* acrylic paints and paintbrush
* thick string or cord
* tape (optional)

WHAT TO DO:

1. Print and cut out the designs you want from page 40. Use a pencil to trace them onto the craft foam. Or you can create your own designs.

#2

#3

2. **Have an adult** cut out the designs with the craft knife.

3. Glue each foam design to a block of wood. Let the glue dry.

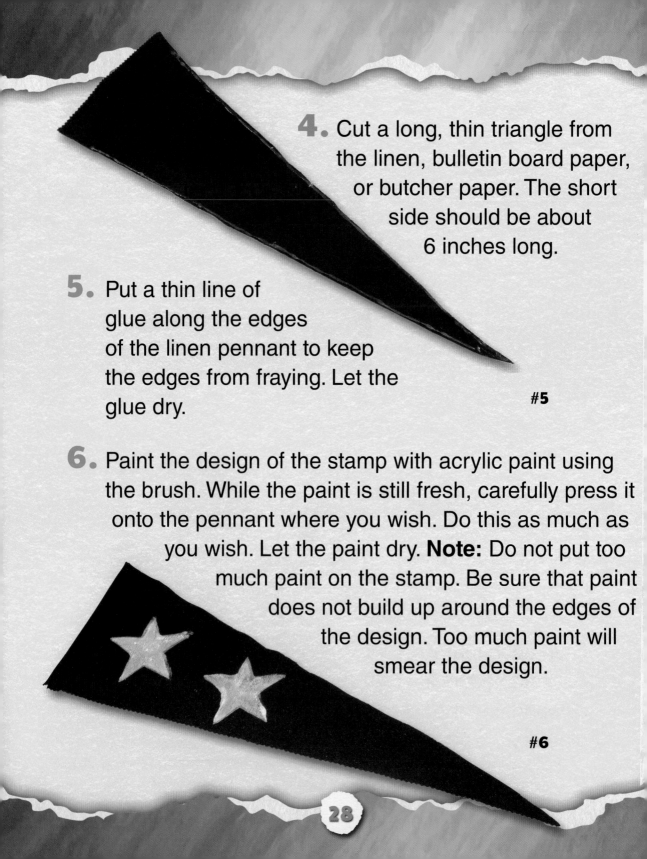

4. Cut a long, thin triangle from the linen, bulletin board paper, or butcher paper. The short side should be about 6 inches long.

5. Put a thin line of glue along the edges of the linen pennant to keep the edges from fraying. Let the glue dry.

#5

6. Paint the design of the stamp with acrylic paint using the brush. While the paint is still fresh, carefully press it onto the pennant where you wish. Do this as much as you wish. Let the paint dry. **Note:** Do not put too much paint on the stamp. Be sure that paint does not build up around the edges of the design. Too much paint will smear the design.

#6

#8

7. To add other colors or designs to the pennant, repeat Step 6 with new designs or colors.

8. Fold about an inch of the short side of the pennant over the string or cord and tape or glue it in place. Space the other pennants out along the cord and fasten them in place. **Have an adult** hang the pennants where they can be enjoyed but are not in the way.

Fish Rod Puppet

Fishing is a popular summer activity. It is something that children and adults can enjoy together. Some people eat the fish they catch. Others let them go. Like people, fish also need oxygen to live. Fish can breathe underwater because they have gills. Gills contain very small blood vessels that are able to take the oxygen out of the water. The fish puppets in this project can be used to do shows on land or to play with in a pool. Be sure to have AN ADULT with you when you play in or near water.

What you will need:

- cleaning sponges—different colors
- scissors
- craft foam—different colors
- pencil
- permanent markers
- craft knife (optional)
- waterproof glue
- a dowel about 12 inches long and ¼ inch thick
- wooden beads with a ¼-inch-wide hole (optional)

WHAT TO DO:

1. Cut a small triangle from the cleaning sponge to form a mouth. Cut away the corners of the sponge to make it look more like a fish.

2. Print and cut out the different fin patterns from page 38. Use a pencil or marker to trace them onto the craft foam.

#1

3. Cut out the fins from the craft foam.

#3

4. **Have an adult** use the craft knife to make small cuts in the foam where the fins will go. Glue the fins into the cuts on the sponge fish body. Let the glue dry.

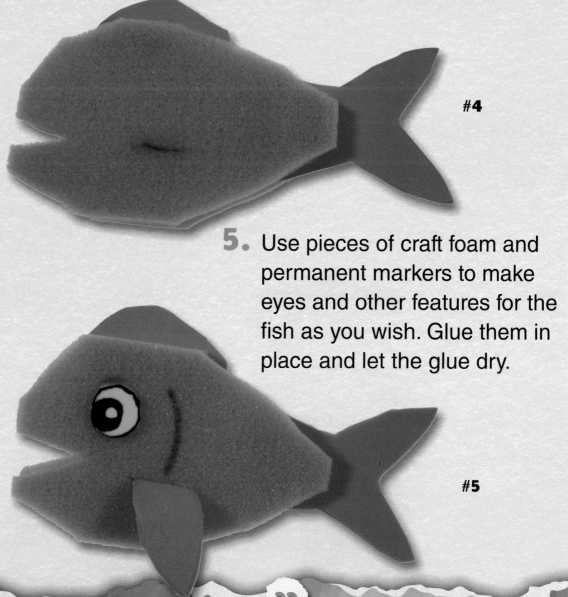

#4

5. Use pieces of craft foam and permanent markers to make eyes and other features for the fish as you wish. Glue them in place and let the glue dry.

#5

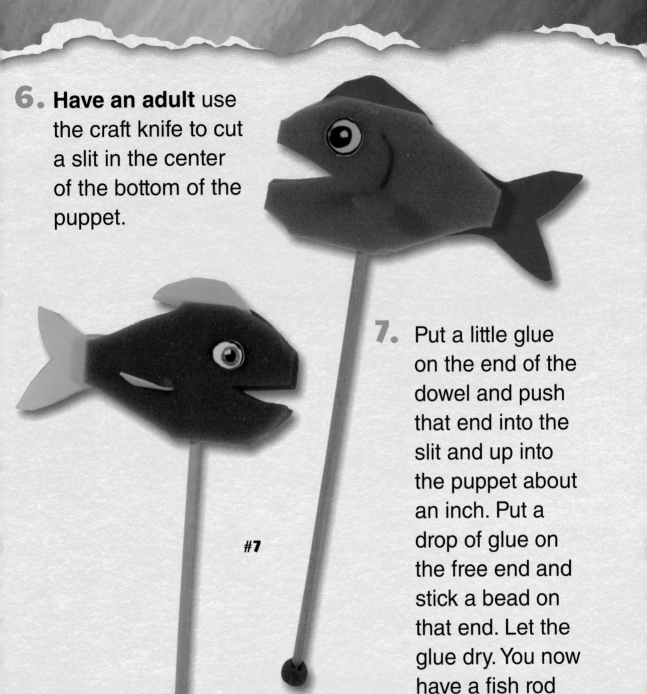

6. **Have an adult** use the craft knife to cut a slit in the center of the bottom of the puppet.

#7

7. Put a little glue on the end of the dowel and push that end into the slit and up into the puppet about an inch. Put a drop of glue on the free end and stick a bead on that end. Let the glue dry. You now have a fish rod puppet!

Tie-Dyed T-Shirt

Summer is the season when people dress for fun in the sun! A tie-dyed T-shirt is just right for wearing on a warm summer day! Tie-dyed clothing became popular in the United States in the 1960s, but people have been tie-dyeing cloth since ancient times. Dyes were made from roots, berries, bark, minerals, and even sea animals. The dyes and dyed cloth were very important items to trade and sell. In 1856, William Perkin, a British scientist, created the first man-made dye for coloring cloth. Have fun dyeing your own shirts with this project!

What you will need:

- plastic sheets or garbage bags
- a white cotton T-shirt
- string or large rubber bands
- three plastic buckets or tubs (4-quart size or larger)
- rubber or latex gloves
- cloth dyes—at least two colors
- two plastic squeeze bottles (optional)
- plastic shopping bags

WHAT TO DO:

1. Cover an outside work area with the plastic sheets or garbage bags to help with the cleanup.

2. Gather the sides of the T-shirt together with your hands. Tie the shirt tightly at the gathered spot with string, or wrap it tightly with a rubber band. Repeat this at least once more in another place on the shirt. **Note:** There are lots of ways to create designs and patterns with tie-dyeing. This way is one of the easiest. You can try different ways.

3. Fill one of the tubs or buckets with clean water. Soak the T-shirt in the water and wring it out.

#2

4. Put on the gloves. Prepare the dyes as directed on the packages. You may put the dyes in the tubs or in the squeeze bottles.

5. a) Dip one end of the T-shirt in one tub of dye or use the squeeze bottle to squirt the dye on the shirt over the tub. Gently squeeze out the excess dye from the shirt. b) Repeat this process with the other color for the other end of the T-shirt.

#5a

#5b

6. Carefully place each dyed end in a plastic shopping bag so that none of the sections touch. Let the T-shirt sit in the bags overnight.

7. The next day, take the bags off the T-shirt, remove the strings or rubber bands, and hang the shirt to dry.

8. Rinse the T-shirt in a tub of cool water and hang it to dry again before you wear it. **Note:** The first or second time you wash the T-shirt, wash it separately in cool water to make sure that the dyes do not get on other clothes.

#8

PATTERNS

The percentages included on the patterns tell you how much to enlarge or shrink the image using a copier. Most copiers and printers have an adjustable size/percentage feature to change the size of an image when you print it. After you print the pattern to its correct size, cut it out. Trace it onto the material listed in the craft.

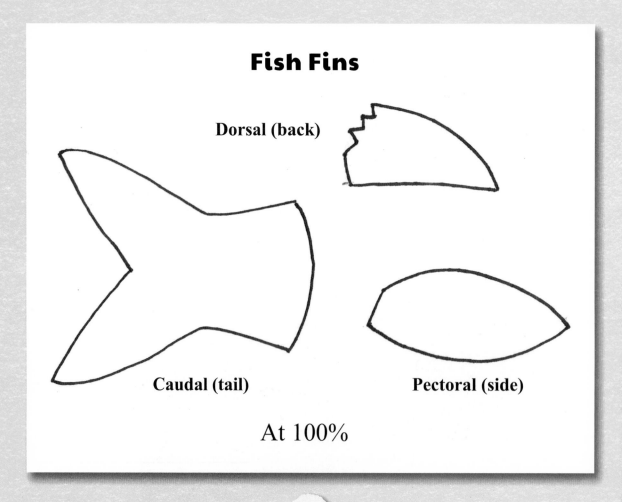

Fish Fins

Dorsal (back)

Caudal (tail)

Pectoral (side)

At 100%

Watermelon Magnet Patterns

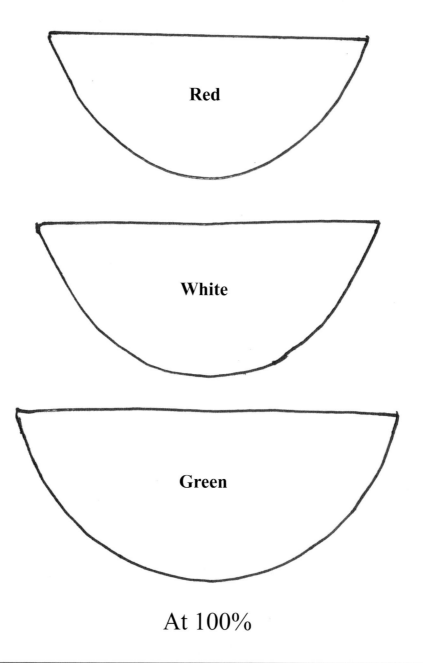

Red

White

Green

At 100%

Rubber Stamps for Pennants

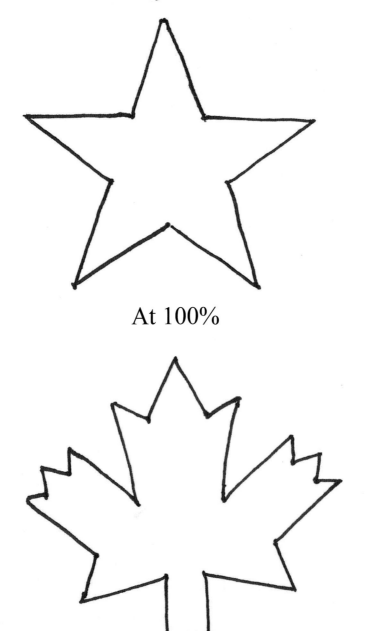

At 100%

Castle Patterns
(The size will depend on the materials used.)

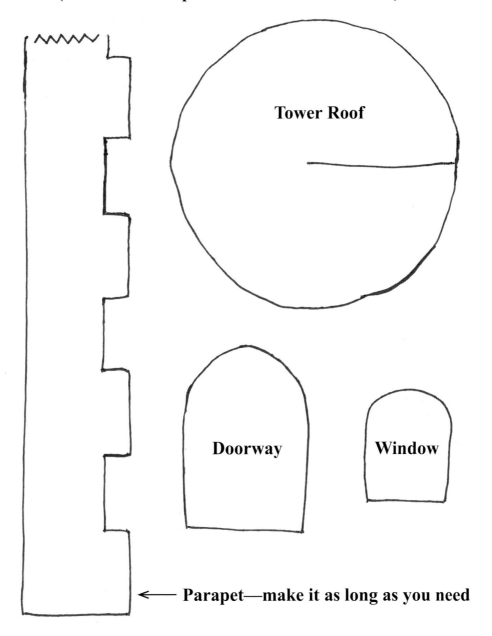

Tower Roof

Doorway

Window

← Parapet—make it as long as you need

Bug Mask

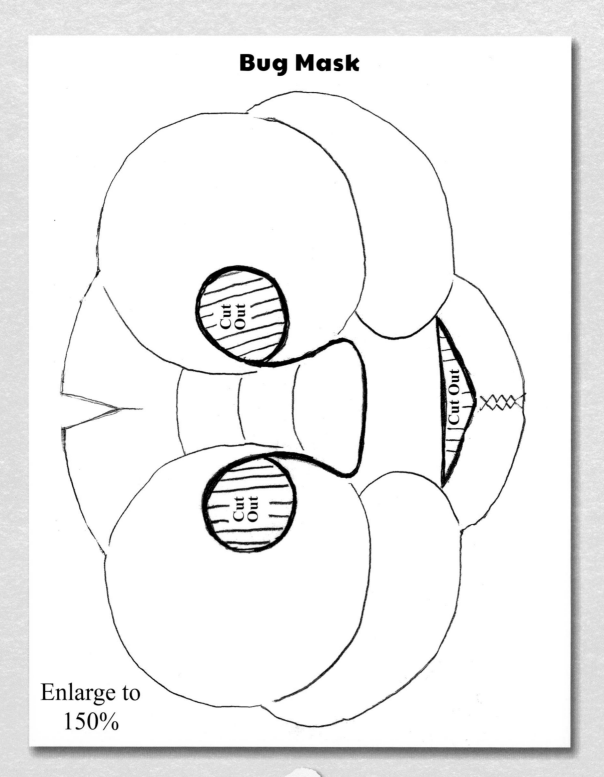

Enlarge to
150%

Bug Mask Parts (optional)

**Eye Ring
(make 2)**

**Antenna
(make 2)**

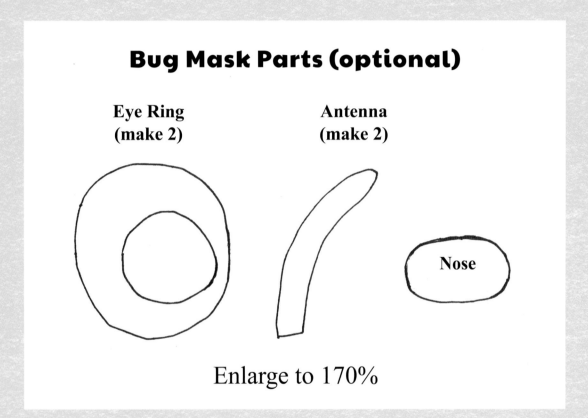

Nose

Enlarge to 170%

Fan

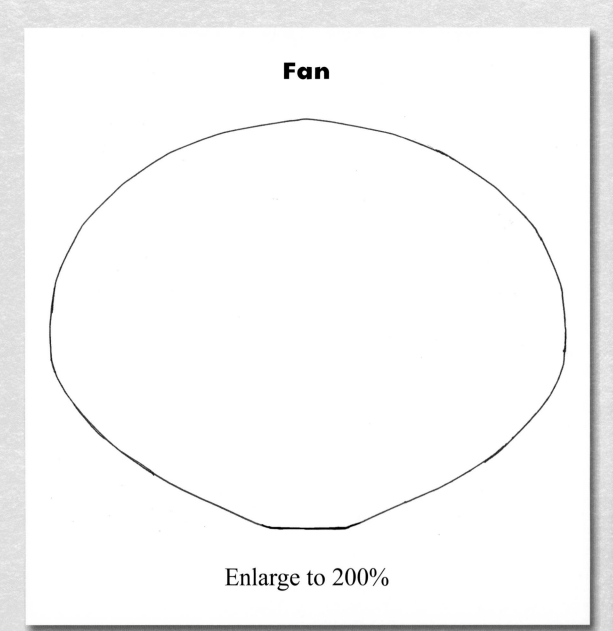

Enlarge to 200%

Read About

Books

Editors of *Make. Make: School's Out Summer Fun.* North Sebastopol, Calif.: Maker Media, Inc., 2012.

Editors of *Martha Stewart Living. Martha Stewart's Favorite Crafts for Kids: 175 Projects for Kids of All Ages to Create, Build, Design, Explore, and Share.* New York: Potter Craft, 2013.

Ross, Kathy. *Step-by-Step Crafts for Summer.* Honesdale, Pa.: Boyds Mills Press, 2007.

Internet Addresses

Spoonful: 401 Summer Crafts

http://spoonful.com/summer/
summer-crafts

DLTK's Crafts for Kids: Summer Crafts for Kids

http://www.dltk-holidays.com/
summer/crafts.htm

Visit Randel McGee's Web site at
http://www.mcgeeproductions.com

INDEX

About the Author

Randel McGee has liked to make things and has played with paper and scissors as long as he can remember. He also likes telling stories and performing. He is an internationally recognized storyteller, ventriloquist, and puppeteer. He and his dragon puppet, Groark, have performed all around the United States and Asia and have appeared in two award-winning video series on character education. He also portrays the famous author Hans Christian Andersen in storytelling performances, where he makes amazing cut-paper designs while he tells stories, just like Andersen did. He likes showing teachers and children the fun they can have with paper projects, storytelling, and puppetry. Randel McGee lives in central California with his wife, Marsha. They have five grown children.